Fun Schway Journal

Maintaining Balance

Feng Shui

Mallory Neeve Wilkins

Fun Schway Journal

Copyright © 2016 Mallory Neeve Wilkins.
All rights reserved.

ISBN-13: 978-1519785190
ISBN-10: 1519785194
BISAC: Literary Collections / Diaries & Journals

This publication is designed to provide inspiration and encouragement in regard to the subject matter covered and is sold with the understanding that the author is not responsible for any reaction to, or action taken or not taken as a result of reading this material.

No part of this publication may be reproduced or transmitted in any form or by any means, electronic, mechanical, photocopying, recording, scanning or otherwise.

Fun Schway Journal

Maintaining Balance

From the ancient teachings of Feng Shui, positive and negative energies surround us within the environment, nature, situations, relationships and material products. Be mindful of Yin/Yang energy by paying attention to details, and then create a positive, healthy lifestyle by recording these differences. Note the time, date (similarities) of repetitive negative situations that require attention and you will attract positive energy: maintaining the balance: Good Fun Schway!

Other books by Author Mallory Neeve Wilkins

Fun Schway Interiors (Reference, How-to)

Ancient Secrets for a Healthy Home (Reference, How-to)

House of the Caduceus (Novel, mystery)

Hot-Walker Life on the Fast Track
(Sports Crime Romance Novel)

Graveyard Autos (Photography)

The Laundry Art Book (Photography)

(Available in ebook & print.)

Fun Schway Journal

A personal journal

to collect insights from your day by identifying the positive and negative activities within your environment, surroundings, relationships, situations and other aspects relative to your feelings, emotions, likes and dislikes. The journal is a place where you can observe repeated actions, pin pictures, list negative situations and note when positive energy creates balance and a state of well-being.

Gratitude, being mindful and aware all help to remove the negative energies that cause havoc and you will begin to feel healthy with more energy, and less stress.
The 'dates' you record will identify a time of year when you experience more Yin than Yang energy – all to do with... maintaining balance – Feng Shui.

Good Fun Schway!

Fun Schway Journal

Maintaining Balance

From the ancient teachings of Feng Shui, positive and negative energies surround us within the environment, nature, situations, relationships and material products. Be mindful of Yin/Yang energy by paying attention to details, and then create a positive, healthy lifestyle by recording these differences. Note the time, date (similarities) of repetitive negative situations that require attention and you will attract positive energy: maintaining the balance: Good Fun Schway!

Date:_____

Gratitude: for the positive Yang energy.

Awareness: negative Yin energy.

Fun Schway Journal

NOTES - comments:

Fun Schway Journal

Maintaining Balance

From the ancient teachings of Feng Shui, positive and negative energies surround us within the environment, nature, situations, relationships and material products. Be mindful of Yin/Yang energy by paying attention to details, and then create a positive, healthy lifestyle by recording these differences. Note the time, date (similarities) of repetitive negative situations that require attention and you will attract positive energy: maintaining the balance: Good Fun Schway!

Date:_____

Gratitude: for the positive Yang energy.

Awareness: negative Yin energy.

Fun Schway Journal

NOTES - comments:

Fun Schway Journal

Maintaining Balance

From the ancient teachings of Feng Shui, positive and negative energies surround us within the environment, nature, situations, relationships and material products. Be mindful of Yin/Yang energy by paying attention to details, and then create a positive, healthy lifestyle by recording these differences. Note the time, date (similarities) of repetitive negative situations that require attention and you will attract positive energy: maintaining the balance: Good Fun Schway!

Date:_____

Gratitude: for the positive Yang energy.

Awareness: negative Yin energy.

Fun Schway Journal

NOTES - comments:

Fun Schway Journal

Maintaining Balance

From the ancient teachings of Feng Shui, positive and negative energies surround us within the environment, nature, situations, relationships and material products. Be mindful of Yin/Yang energy by paying attention to details, and then create a positive, healthy lifestyle by recording these differences. Note the time, date (similarities) of repetitive negative situations that require attention and you will attract positive energy: maintaining the balance: Good Fun Schway!

Date:_____

Gratitude: for the positive Yang energy.

Awareness: negative Yin energy.

Fun Schway Journal

NOTES - comments:

Fun Schway Journal

Maintaining Balance

From the ancient teachings of Feng Shui, positive and negative energies surround us within the environment, nature, situations, relationships and material products. Be mindful of Yin/Yang energy by paying attention to details, and then create a positive, healthy lifestyle by recording these differences. Note the time, date (similarities) of repetitive negative situations that require attention and you will attract positive energy: maintaining the balance: Good Fun Schway!

Date:_____

Gratitude: for the positive Yang energy.

Awareness: negative Yin energy.

Fun Schway Journal

NOTES - comments:

Fun Schway Journal

Maintaining Balance

From the ancient teachings of Feng Shui, positive and negative energies surround us within the environment, nature, situations, relationships and material products. Be mindful of Yin/Yang energy by paying attention to details, and then create a positive, healthy lifestyle by recording these differences. Note the time, date (similarities) of repetitive negative situations that require attention and you will attract positive energy: maintaining the balance: Good Fun Schway!

Date:_____

Gratitude: for the positive Yang energy.

Awareness: negative Yin energy.

Fun Schway Journal

NOTES - comments:

Fun Schway Journal

Maintaining Balance

From the ancient teachings of Feng Shui, positive and negative energies surround us within the environment, nature, situations, relationships and material products. Be mindful of Yin/Yang energy by paying attention to details, and then create a positive, healthy lifestyle by recording these differences. Note the time, date (similarities) of repetitive negative situations that require attention and you will attract positive energy: maintaining the balance: Good Fun Schway!

Date:_____

Gratitude: for the positive Yang energy.

Awareness: negative Yin energy.

Fun Schway Journal

NOTES - comments:

Fun Schway Journal

Maintaining Balance

From the ancient teachings of Feng Shui, positive and negative energies surround us within the environment, nature, situations, relationships and material products. Be mindful of Yin/Yang energy by paying attention to details, and then create a positive, healthy lifestyle by recording these differences. Note the time, date (similarities) of repetitive negative situations that require attention and you will attract positive energy: maintaining the balance: Good Fun Schway!

Date:_____

Gratitude: for the positive Yang energy.

Awareness: negative Yin energy.

Fun Schway Journal

NOTES - comments:

Fun Schway Journal

Maintaining Balance

From the ancient teachings of Feng Shui, positive and negative energies surround us within the environment, nature, situations, relationships and material products. Be mindful of Yin/Yang energy by paying attention to details, and then create a positive, healthy lifestyle by recording these differences. Note the time, date (similarities) of repetitive negative situations that require attention and you will attract positive energy: maintaining the balance: Good Fun Schway!

Date:_____

Gratitude: for the positive Yang energy.

Awareness: negative Yin energy.

Fun Schway Journal

NOTES - comments:

Fun Schway Journal

Maintaining Balance

From the ancient teachings of Feng Shui, positive and negative energies surround us within the environment, nature, situations, relationships and material products. Be mindful of Yin/Yang energy by paying attention to details, and then create a positive, healthy lifestyle by recording these differences. Note the time, date (similarities) of repetitive negative situations that require attention and you will attract positive energy: maintaining the balance: Good Fun Schway!

Date:_____

Gratitude: for the positive Yang energy.

Awareness: negative Yin energy.

Fun Schway Journal

NOTES - comments:

Fun Schway Journal

Maintaining Balance

From the ancient teachings of Feng Shui, positive and negative energies surround us within the environment, nature, situations, relationships and material products. Be mindful of Yin/Yang energy by paying attention to details, and then create a positive, healthy lifestyle by recording these differences. Note the time, date (similarities) of repetitive negative situations that require attention and you will attract positive energy: maintaining the balance: Good Fun Schway!

Date:_____

Gratitude: for the positive Yang energy.

Awareness: negative Yin energy.

Fun Schway Journal

NOTES - comments:

Fun Schway Journal

Maintaining Balance

From the ancient teachings of Feng Shui, positive and negative energies surround us within the environment, nature, situations, relationships and material products. Be mindful of Yin/Yang energy by paying attention to details, and then create a positive, healthy lifestyle by recording these differences. Note the time, date (similarities) of repetitive negative situations that require attention and you will attract positive energy: maintaining the balance: Good Fun Schway!

Date:_____

Gratitude: for the positive Yang energy.

Awareness: negative Yin energy.

Fun Schway Journal

NOTES - comments:

Fun Schway Journal

Maintaining Balance

From the ancient teachings of Feng Shui, positive and negative energies surround us within the environment, nature, situations, relationships and material products. Be mindful of Yin/Yang energy by paying attention to details, and then create a positive, healthy lifestyle by recording these differences. Note the time, date (similarities) of repetitive negative situations that require attention and you will attract positive energy: maintaining the balance: Good Fun Schway!

Date:_____

Gratitude: for the positive Yang energy.

Awareness: negative Yin energy.

Fun Schway Journal

NOTES - comments:

Fun Schway Journal

Maintaining Balance

From the ancient teachings of Feng Shui, positive and negative energies surround us within the environment, nature, situations, relationships and material products. Be mindful of Yin/Yang energy by paying attention to details, and then create a positive, healthy lifestyle by recording these differences. Note the time, date (similarities) of repetitive negative situations that require attention and you will attract positive energy: maintaining the balance: Good Fun Schway!

Date:_____

Gratitude: for the positive Yang energy.

Awareness: negative Yin energy.

Fun Schway Journal

NOTES - comments:

Fun Schway Journal

Maintaining Balance

From the ancient teachings of Feng Shui, positive and negative energies surround us within the environment, nature, situations, relationships and material products. Be mindful of Yin/Yang energy by paying attention to details, and then create a positive, healthy lifestyle by recording these differences. Note the time, date (similarities) of repetitive negative situations that require attention and you will attract positive energy: maintaining the balance: Good Fun Schway!

Date:_____

Gratitude: for the positive Yang energy.

Awareness: negative Yin energy.

Fun Schway Journal

NOTES - comments:

Fun Schway Journal

Maintaining Balance

From the ancient teachings of Feng Shui, positive and negative energies surround us within the environment, nature, situations, relationships and material products. Be mindful of Yin/Yang energy by paying attention to details, and then create a positive, healthy lifestyle by recording these differences. Note the time, date (similarities) of repetitive negative situations that require attention and you will attract positive energy: maintaining the balance: Good Fun Schway!

Date:_____

Gratitude: for the positive Yang energy.

Awareness: negative Yin energy.

Fun Schway Journal

NOTES - comments:

Fun Schway Journal

Maintaining Balance

From the ancient teachings of Feng Shui, positive and negative energies surround us within the environment, nature, situations, relationships and material products. Be mindful of Yin/Yang energy by paying attention to details, and then create a positive, healthy lifestyle by recording these differences. Note the time, date (similarities) of repetitive negative situations that require attention and you will attract positive energy: maintaining the balance: Good Fun Schway!

Date:_____

Gratitude: for the positive Yang energy.

Awareness: negative Yin energy.

Fun Schway Journal

NOTES - comments:

Fun Schway Journal

Maintaining Balance

From the ancient teachings of Feng Shui, positive and negative energies surround us within the environment, nature, situations, relationships and material products. Be mindful of Yin/Yang energy by paying attention to details, and then create a positive, healthy lifestyle by recording these differences. Note the time, date (similarities) of repetitive negative situations that require attention and you will attract positive energy: maintaining the balance: Good Fun Schway!

Date:_____

Gratitude: for the positive Yang energy.

Awareness: negative Yin energy.

Fun Schway Journal

NOTES - comments:

Fun Schway Journal

Maintaining Balance

From the ancient teachings of Feng Shui, positive and negative energies surround us within the environment, nature, situations, relationships and material products. Be mindful of Yin/Yang energy by paying attention to details, and then create a positive, healthy lifestyle by recording these differences. Note the time, date (similarities) of repetitive negative situations that require attention and you will attract positive energy: maintaining the balance: Good Fun Schway!

Date:_____

Gratitude: for the positive Yang energy.

Awareness: negative Yin energy.

Fun Schway Journal

NOTES - comments:

Fun Schway Journal

Maintaining Balance

From the ancient teachings of Feng Shui, positive and negative energies surround us within the environment, nature, situations, relationships and material products. Be mindful of Yin/Yang energy by paying attention to details, and then create a positive, healthy lifestyle by recording these differences. Note the time, date (similarities) of repetitive negative situations that require attention and you will attract positive energy: maintaining the balance: Good Fun Schway!

Date:_____

Gratitude: for the positive Yang energy.

Awareness: negative Yin energy.

Fun Schway Journal

NOTES - comments:

Fun Schway Journal

Maintaining Balance

From the ancient teachings of Feng Shui, positive and negative energies surround us within the environment, nature, situations, relationships and material products. Be mindful of Yin/Yang energy by paying attention to details, and then create a positive, healthy lifestyle by recording these differences. Note the time, date (similarities) of repetitive negative situations that require attention and you will attract positive energy: maintaining the balance: Good Fun Schway!

Date:_____

Gratitude: for the positive Yang energy.

Awareness: negative Yin energy.

Fun Schway Journal

NOTES - comments:

Fun Schway Journal

Maintaining Balance

From the ancient teachings of Feng Shui, positive and negative energies surround us within the environment, nature, situations, relationships and material products. Be mindful of Yin/Yang energy by paying attention to details, and then create a positive, healthy lifestyle by recording these differences. Note the time, date (similarities) of repetitive negative situations that require attention and you will attract positive energy: maintaining the balance: Good Fun Schway!

Date:_____

Gratitude: for the positive Yang energy.

Awareness: negative Yin energy.

Fun Schway Journal

NOTES - comments:

Fun Schway Journal

Maintaining Balance

From the ancient teachings of Feng Shui, positive and negative energies surround us within the environment, nature, situations, relationships and material products. Be mindful of Yin/Yang energy by paying attention to details, and then create a positive, healthy lifestyle by recording these differences. Note the time, date (similarities) of repetitive negative situations that require attention and you will attract positive energy: maintaining the balance: Good Fun Schway!

Date:_____

Gratitude: for the positive Yang energy.

Awareness: negative Yin energy.

Fun Schway Journal

NOTES - comments:

Fun Schway Journal

Maintaining Balance

From the ancient teachings of Feng Shui, positive and negative energies surround us within the environment, nature, situations, relationships and material products. Be mindful of Yin/Yang energy by paying attention to details, and then create a positive, healthy lifestyle by recording these differences. Note the time, date (similarities) of repetitive negative situations that require attention and you will attract positive energy: maintaining the balance: Good Fun Schway!

Date:_____

Gratitude: for the positive Yang energy.

Awareness: negative Yin energy.

Fun Schway Journal

NOTES - comments:

Fun Schway Journal

Maintaining Balance

From the ancient teachings of Feng Shui, positive and negative energies surround us within the environment, nature, situations, relationships and material products. Be mindful of Yin/Yang energy by paying attention to details, and then create a positive, healthy lifestyle by recording these differences. Note the time, date (similarities) of repetitive negative situations that require attention and you will attract positive energy: maintaining the balance: Good Fun Schway!

Date:_____

Gratitude: for the positive Yang energy.

Awareness: negative Yin energy.

Fun Schway Journal

NOTES - comments:

Fun Schway Journal

Maintaining Balance

From the ancient teachings of Feng Shui, positive and negative energies surround us within the environment, nature, situations, relationships and material products. Be mindful of Yin/Yang energy by paying attention to details, and then create a positive, healthy lifestyle by recording these differences. Note the time, date (similarities) of repetitive negative situations that require attention and you will attract positive energy: maintaining the balance: Good Fun Schway!

Date:_____

Gratitude: for the positive Yang energy.

Awareness: negative Yin energy.

Fun Schway Journal

NOTES - comments:

Fun Schway Journal

Maintaining Balance

From the ancient teachings of Feng Shui, positive and negative energies surround us within the environment, nature, situations, relationships and material products. Be mindful of Yin/Yang energy by paying attention to details, and then create a positive, healthy lifestyle by recording these differences. Note the time, date (similarities) of repetitive negative situations that require attention and you will attract positive energy: maintaining the balance: Good Fun Schway!

Date:_____

Gratitude: for the positive Yang energy.

Awareness: negative Yin energy.

Fun Schway Journal

NOTES - comments:

Fun Schway Journal

Maintaining Balance

From the ancient teachings of Feng Shui, positive and negative energies surround us within the environment, nature, situations, relationships and material products. Be mindful of Yin/Yang energy by paying attention to details, and then create a positive, healthy lifestyle by recording these differences. Note the time, date (similarities) of repetitive negative situations that require attention and you will attract positive energy: maintaining the balance: Good Fun Schway!

Date:_____

Gratitude: for the positive Yang energy.

Awareness: negative Yin energy.

Fun Schway Journal

NOTES - comments:

Fun Schway Journal

Maintaining Balance

From the ancient teachings of Feng Shui, positive and negative energies surround us within the environment, nature, situations, relationships and material products. Be mindful of Yin/Yang energy by paying attention to details, and then create a positive, healthy lifestyle by recording these differences. Note the time, date (similarities) of repetitive negative situations that require attention and you will attract positive energy: maintaining the balance: Good Fun Schway!

Date:_____

Gratitude: for the positive Yang energy.

Awareness: negative Yin energy.

Fun Schway Journal

NOTES - comments:

Fun Schway Journal

Maintaining Balance

From the ancient teachings of Feng Shui, positive and negative energies surround us within the environment, nature, situations, relationships and material products. Be mindful of Yin/Yang energy by paying attention to details, and then create a positive, healthy lifestyle by recording these differences. Note the time, date (similarities) of repetitive negative situations that require attention and you will attract positive energy: maintaining the balance: Good Fun Schway!

Date:_____

Gratitude: for the positive Yang energy.

Awareness: negative Yin energy.

Fun Schway Journal

NOTES - comments:

Fun Schway Journal

Maintaining Balance

From the ancient teachings of Feng Shui, positive and negative energies surround us within the environment, nature, situations, relationships and material products. Be mindful of Yin/Yang energy by paying attention to details, and then create a positive, healthy lifestyle by recording these differences. Note the time, date (similarities) of repetitive negative situations that require attention and you will attract positive energy: maintaining the balance: Good Fun Schway!

Date:_____

Gratitude: for the positive Yang energy.

Awareness: negative Yin energy.

Fun Schway Journal

NOTES - comments:

Fun Schway Journal

Maintaining Balance

From the ancient teachings of Feng Shui, positive and negative energies surround us within the environment, nature, situations, relationships and material products. Be mindful of Yin/Yang energy by paying attention to details, and then create a positive, healthy lifestyle by recording these differences. Note the time, date (similarities) of repetitive negative situations that require attention and you will attract positive energy: maintaining the balance: Good Fun Schway!

Date:_____

Gratitude: for the positive Yang energy.

Awareness: negative Yin energy.

Fun Schway Journal

NOTES - comments:

Fun Schway Journal

Maintaining Balance

From the ancient teachings of Feng Shui, positive and negative energies surround us within the environment, nature, situations, relationships and material products. Be mindful of Yin/Yang energy by paying attention to details, and then create a positive, healthy lifestyle by recording these differences. Note the time, date (similarities) of repetitive negative situations that require attention and you will attract positive energy: maintaining the balance: Good Fun Schway!

Date:_____

Gratitude: for the positive Yang energy.

Awareness: negative Yin energy.

Fun Schway Journal

NOTES - comments:

Fun Schway Journal

Maintaining Balance

From the ancient teachings of Feng Shui, positive and negative energies surround us within the environment, nature, situations, relationships and material products. Be mindful of Yin/Yang energy by paying attention to details, and then create a positive, healthy lifestyle by recording these differences. Note the time, date (similarities) of repetitive negative situations that require attention and you will attract positive energy: maintaining the balance: Good Fun Schway!

Date:_____

Gratitude: for the positive Yang energy.

Awareness: negative Yin energy.

Fun Schway Journal

NOTES - comments:

Fun Schway Journal

Maintaining Balance

From the ancient teachings of Feng Shui, positive and negative energies surround us within the environment, nature, situations, relationships and material products. Be mindful of Yin/Yang energy by paying attention to details, and then create a positive, healthy lifestyle by recording these differences. Note the time, date (similarities) of repetitive negative situations that require attention and you will attract positive energy: maintaining the balance: Good Fun Schway!

Date:_____

Gratitude: for the positive Yang energy.

Awareness: negative Yin energy.

Fun Schway Journal

NOTES - comments:

Fun Schway Journal

Maintaining Balance

From the ancient teachings of Feng Shui, positive and negative energies surround us within the environment, nature, situations, relationships and material products. Be mindful of Yin/Yang energy by paying attention to details, and then create a positive, healthy lifestyle by recording these differences. Note the time, date (similarities) of repetitive negative situations that require attention and you will attract positive energy: maintaining the balance: Good Fun Schway!

Date:_____

Gratitude: for the positive Yang energy.

Awareness: negative Yin energy.

Fun Schway Journal

NOTES - comments:

Fun Schway Journal

Maintaining Balance

From the ancient teachings of Feng Shui, positive and negative energies surround us within the environment, nature, situations, relationships and material products. Be mindful of Yin/Yang energy by paying attention to details, and then create a positive, healthy lifestyle by recording these differences. Note the time, date (similarities) of repetitive negative situations that require attention and you will attract positive energy: maintaining the balance: Good Fun Schway!

Date:_____

Gratitude: for the positive Yang energy.

Awareness: negative Yin energy.

Fun Schway Journal

NOTES - comments:

Fun Schway Journal

Maintaining Balance

From the ancient teachings of Feng Shui, positive and negative energies surround us within the environment, nature, situations, relationships and material products. Be mindful of Yin/Yang energy by paying attention to details, and then create a positive, healthy lifestyle by recording these differences. Note the time, date (similarities) of repetitive negative situations that require attention and you will attract positive energy: maintaining the balance: Good Fun Schway!

Date:_____

Gratitude: for the positive Yang energy.

Awareness: negative Yin energy.

Fun Schway Journal

NOTES - comments:

Fun Schway Journal

Maintaining Balance

From the ancient teachings of Feng Shui, positive and negative energies surround us within the environment, nature, situations, relationships and material products. Be mindful of Yin/Yang energy by paying attention to details, and then create a positive, healthy lifestyle by recording these differences. Note the time, date (similarities) of repetitive negative situations that require attention and you will attract positive energy: maintaining the balance: Good Fun Schway!

Date:_____

Gratitude: for the positive Yang energy.

Awareness: negative Yin energy.

Fun Schway Journal

NOTES - comments:

Fun Schway Journal

Maintaining Balance

From the ancient teachings of Feng Shui, positive and negative energies surround us within the environment, nature, situations, relationships and material products. Be mindful of Yin/Yang energy by paying attention to details, and then create a positive, healthy lifestyle by recording these differences. Note the time, date (similarities) of repetitive negative situations that require attention and you will attract positive energy: maintaining the balance: Good Fun Schway!

Date:_____

Gratitude: for the positive Yang energy.

Awareness: negative Yin energy.

Fun Schway Journal

NOTES - comments:

Fun Schway Journal

Maintaining Balance

From the ancient teachings of Feng Shui, positive and negative energies surround us within the environment, nature, situations, relationships and material products. Be mindful of Yin/Yang energy by paying attention to details, and then create a positive, healthy lifestyle by recording these differences. Note the time, date (similarities) of repetitive negative situations that require attention and you will attract positive energy: maintaining the balance: Good Fun Schway!

Date:_____

Gratitude: for the positive Yang energy.

Awareness: negative Yin energy.

Fun Schway Journal

NOTES - comments:

Fun Schway Journal

Maintaining Balance

From the ancient teachings of Feng Shui, positive and negative energies surround us within the environment, nature, situations, relationships and material products. Be mindful of Yin/Yang energy by paying attention to details, and then create a positive, healthy lifestyle by recording these differences. Note the time, date (similarities) of repetitive negative situations that require attention and you will attract positive energy: maintaining the balance: Good Fun Schway!

Date:_____

Gratitude: for the positive Yang energy.

Awareness: negative Yin energy.

Fun Schway Journal

NOTES - comments:

Fun Schway Journal

Maintaining Balance

From the ancient teachings of Feng Shui, positive and negative energies surround us within the environment, nature, situations, relationships and material products. Be mindful of Yin/Yang energy by paying attention to details, and then create a positive, healthy lifestyle by recording these differences. Note the time, date (similarities) of repetitive negative situations that require attention and you will attract positive energy: maintaining the balance: Good Fun Schway!

Date:_____

Gratitude: for the positive Yang energy.

Awareness: negative Yin energy.

Fun Schway Journal

NOTES - comments:

Fun Schway Journal

Maintaining Balance

From the ancient teachings of Feng Shui, positive and negative energies surround us within the environment, nature, situations, relationships and material products. Be mindful of Yin/Yang energy by paying attention to details, and then create a positive, healthy lifestyle by recording these differences. Note the time, date (similarities) of repetitive negative situations that require attention and you will attract positive energy: maintaining the balance: Good Fun Schway!

Date:_____

Gratitude: for the positive Yang energy.

Awareness: negative Yin energy.

Fun Schway Journal

NOTES - comments:

Fun Schway Journal

Maintaining Balance

From the ancient teachings of Feng Shui, positive and negative energies surround us within the environment, nature, situations, relationships and material products. Be mindful of Yin/Yang energy by paying attention to details, and then create a positive, healthy lifestyle by recording these differences. Note the time, date (similarities) of repetitive negative situations that require attention and you will attract positive energy: maintaining the balance: Good Fun Schway!

Date:_____

Gratitude: for the positive Yang energy.

Awareness: negative Yin energy.

Fun Schway Journal

NOTES - comments:

Fun Schway Journal
Maintaining Balance

From the ancient teachings of Feng Shui, positive and negative energies surround us within the environment, nature, situations, relationships and material products. Be mindful of Yin/Yang energy by paying attention to details, and then create a positive, healthy lifestyle by recording these differences. Note the time, date (similarities) of repetitive negative situations that require attention and you will attract positive energy: maintaining the balance: Good Fun Schway!

Date:_____

Gratitude: for the positive Yang energy.

Awareness: negative Yin energy.

Fun Schway Journal

NOTES - comments:

Fun Schway Journal

Maintaining Balance

From the ancient teachings of Feng Shui, positive and negative energies surround us within the environment, nature, situations, relationships and material products. Be mindful of Yin/Yang energy by paying attention to details, and then create a positive, healthy lifestyle by recording these differences. Note the time, date (similarities) of repetitive negative situations that require attention and you will attract positive energy: maintaining the balance: Good Fun Schway!

Date:_____

Gratitude: for the positive Yang energy.

Awareness: negative Yin energy.

Fun Schway Journal

NOTES - comments:

Fun Schway Journal

Maintaining Balance

From the ancient teachings of Feng Shui, positive and negative energies surround us within the environment, nature, situations, relationships and material products. Be mindful of Yin/Yang energy by paying attention to details, and then create a positive, healthy lifestyle by recording these differences. Note the time, date (similarities) of repetitive negative situations that require attention and you will attract positive energy: maintaining the balance: Good Fun Schway!

Date:_____

Gratitude: for the positive Yang energy.

Awareness: negative Yin energy.

Fun Schway Journal

NOTES - comments:

Fun Schway Journal

Maintaining Balance

From the ancient teachings of Feng Shui, positive and negative energies surround us within the environment, nature, situations, relationships and material products. Be mindful of Yin/Yang energy by paying attention to details, and then create a positive, healthy lifestyle by recording these differences. Note the time, date (similarities) of repetitive negative situations that require attention and you will attract positive energy: maintaining the balance: Good Fun Schway!

Date:_____

Gratitude: for the positive Yang energy.

Awareness: negative Yin energy.

Fun Schway Journal

NOTES - comments:

Fun Schway Journal

Maintaining Balance

From the ancient teachings of Feng Shui, positive and negative energies surround us within the environment, nature, situations, relationships and material products. Be mindful of Yin/Yang energy by paying attention to details, and then create a positive, healthy lifestyle by recording these differences. Note the time, date (similarities) of repetitive negative situations that require attention and you will attract positive energy: maintaining the balance: Good Fun Schway!

Date:_____

Gratitude: for the positive Yang energy.

Awareness: negative Yin energy.

Fun Schway Journal

NOTES - comments:

Fun Schway Journal

Maintaining Balance

From the ancient teachings of Feng Shui, positive and negative energies surround us within the environment, nature, situations, relationships and material products. Be mindful of Yin/Yang energy by paying attention to details, and then create a positive, healthy lifestyle by recording these differences. Note the time, date (similarities) of repetitive negative situations that require attention and you will attract positive energy: maintaining the balance: Good Fun Schway!

Date:_____

Gratitude: for the positive Yang energy.

Awareness: negative Yin energy.

Fun Schway Journal

NOTES - comments:

Fun Schway Journal

Maintaining Balance

From the ancient teachings of Feng Shui, positive and negative energies surround us within the environment, nature, situations, relationships and material products. Be mindful of Yin/Yang energy by paying attention to details, and then create a positive, healthy lifestyle by recording these differences. Note the time, date (similarities) of repetitive negative situations that require attention and you will attract positive energy: maintaining the balance: Good Fun Schway!

Date:_____

Gratitude: for the positive Yang energy.

Awareness: negative Yin energy.

Fun Schway Journal

NOTES - comments:

Fun Schway Journal

Maintaining Balance

From the ancient teachings of Feng Shui, positive and negative energies surround us within the environment, nature, situations, relationships and material products. Be mindful of Yin/Yang energy by paying attention to details, and then create a positive, healthy lifestyle by recording these differences. Note the time, date (similarities) of repetitive negative situations that require attention and you will attract positive energy: maintaining the balance: Good Fun Schway!

Date:_____

Gratitude: for the positive Yang energy.

Awareness: negative Yin energy.

Fun Schway Journal

NOTES - comments:

Fun Schway Journal

Maintaining Balance

From the ancient teachings of Feng Shui, positive and negative energies surround us within the environment, nature, situations, relationships and material products. Be mindful of Yin/Yang energy by paying attention to details, and then create a positive, healthy lifestyle by recording these differences. Note the time, date (similarities) of repetitive negative situations that require attention and you will attract positive energy: maintaining the balance: Good Fun Schway!

Date:_____

Gratitude: for the positive Yang energy.

Awareness: negative Yin energy.

Fun Schway Journal

NOTES - comments:

Fun Schway Journal

Maintaining Balance

From the ancient teachings of Feng Shui, positive and negative energies surround us within the environment, nature, situations, relationships and material products. Be mindful of Yin/Yang energy by paying attention to details, and then create a positive, healthy lifestyle by recording these differences. Note the time, date (similarities) of repetitive negative situations that require attention and you will attract positive energy: maintaining the balance: Good Fun Schway!

Date:_____

Gratitude: for the positive Yang energy.

Awareness: negative Yin energy.

Fun Schway Journal

NOTES - comments:

Fun Schway Journal

Maintaining Balance

From the ancient teachings of Feng Shui, positive and negative energies surround us within the environment, nature, situations, relationships and material products. Be mindful of Yin/Yang energy by paying attention to details, and then create a positive, healthy lifestyle by recording these differences. Note the time, date (similarities) of repetitive negative situations that require attention and you will attract positive energy: maintaining the balance: Good Fun Schway!

Date:_____

Gratitude: for the positive Yang energy.

Awareness: negative Yin energy.

Fun Schway Journal

NOTES - comments:

Fun Schway Journal

Maintaining Balance

From the ancient teachings of Feng Shui, positive and negative energies surround us within the environment, nature, situations, relationships and material products. Be mindful of Yin/Yang energy by paying attention to details, and then create a positive, healthy lifestyle by recording these differences. Note the time, date (similarities) of repetitive negative situations that require attention and you will attract positive energy: maintaining the balance: Good Fun Schway!

Date:_____

Gratitude: for the positive Yang energy.

Awareness: negative Yin energy.

Fun Schway Journal

NOTES - comments:

Fun Schway Journal

Maintaining Balance

From the ancient teachings of Feng Shui, positive and negative energies surround us within the environment, nature, situations, relationships and material products. Be mindful of Yin/Yang energy by paying attention to details, and then create a positive, healthy lifestyle by recording these differences. Note the time, date (similarities) of repetitive negative situations that require attention and you will attract positive energy: maintaining the balance: Good Fun Schway!

Date:_____

Gratitude: for the positive Yang energy.

Awareness: negative Yin energy.

Fun Schway Journal

NOTES - comments:

Fun Schway Journal

Maintaining Balance

From the ancient teachings of Feng Shui, positive and negative energies surround us within the environment, nature, situations, relationships and material products. Be mindful of Yin/Yang energy by paying attention to details, and then create a positive, healthy lifestyle by recording these differences. Note the time, date (similarities) of repetitive negative situations that require attention and you will attract positive energy: maintaining the balance: Good Fun Schway!

Date:_____

Gratitude: for the positive Yang energy.

Awareness: negative Yin energy.

Fun Schway Journal

NOTES - comments:

Fun Schway Journal

Maintaining Balance

From the ancient teachings of Feng Shui, positive and negative energies surround us within the environment, nature, situations, relationships and material products. Be mindful of Yin/Yang energy by paying attention to details, and then create a positive, healthy lifestyle by recording these differences. Note the time, date (similarities) of repetitive negative situations that require attention and you will attract positive energy: maintaining the balance: Good Fun Schway!

Date:_____

Gratitude: for the positive Yang energy.

Awareness: negative Yin energy.

Fun Schway Journal

NOTES - comments:

Fun Schway Journal

Maintaining Balance

From the ancient teachings of Feng Shui, positive and negative energies surround us within the environment, nature, situations, relationships and material products. Be mindful of Yin/Yang energy by paying attention to details, and then create a positive, healthy lifestyle by recording these differences. Note the time, date (similarities) of repetitive negative situations that require attention and you will attract positive energy: maintaining the balance: Good Fun Schway!

Date:_____

Gratitude: for the positive Yang energy.

Awareness: negative Yin energy.

Fun Schway Journal

NOTES - comments:

Fun Schway Journal

Maintaining Balance

From the ancient teachings of Feng Shui, positive and negative energies surround us within the environment, nature, situations, relationships and material products. Be mindful of Yin/Yang energy by paying attention to details, and then create a positive, healthy lifestyle by recording these differences. Note the time, date (similarities) of repetitive negative situations that require attention and you will attract positive energy: maintaining the balance: Good Fun Schway!

Date:_____

Gratitude: for the positive Yang energy.

Awareness: negative Yin energy.

Fun Schway Journal

NOTES - comments:

Fun Schway Journal

Maintaining Balance

From the ancient teachings of Feng Shui, positive and negative energies surround us within the environment, nature, situations, relationships and material products. Be mindful of Yin/Yang energy by paying attention to details, and then create a positive, healthy lifestyle by recording these differences. Note the time, date (similarities) of repetitive negative situations that require attention and you will attract positive energy: maintaining the balance: Good Fun Schway!

Date:_____

Gratitude: for the positive Yang energy.

Awareness: negative Yin energy.

Fun Schway Journal

NOTES - comments:

Fun Schway Journal

Maintaining Balance

From the ancient teachings of Feng Shui, positive and negative energies surround us within the environment, nature, situations, relationships and material products. Be mindful of Yin/Yang energy by paying attention to details, and then create a positive, healthy lifestyle by recording these differences. Note the time, date (similarities) of repetitive negative situations that require attention and you will attract positive energy: maintaining the balance: Good Fun Schway!

Date:_____

Gratitude: for the positive Yang energy.

Awareness: negative Yin energy.

Fun Schway Journal

NOTES - comments:

Fun Schway Journal

Maintaining Balance

From the ancient teachings of Feng Shui, positive and negative energies surround us within the environment, nature, situations, relationships and material products. Be mindful of Yin/Yang energy by paying attention to details, and then create a positive, healthy lifestyle by recording these differences. Note the time, date (similarities) of repetitive negative situations that require attention and you will attract positive energy: maintaining the balance: Good Fun Schway!

Date:_____

Gratitude: for the positive Yang energy.

Awareness: negative Yin energy.

Fun Schway Journal

NOTES - comments:

Fun Schway Journal

Maintaining Balance

From the ancient teachings of Feng Shui, positive and negative energies surround us within the environment, nature, situations, relationships and material products. Be mindful of Yin/Yang energy by paying attention to details, and then create a positive, healthy lifestyle by recording these differences. Note the time, date (similarities) of repetitive negative situations that require attention and you will attract positive energy: maintaining the balance: Good Fun Schway!

Date:_____

Gratitude: for the positive Yang energy.

Awareness: negative Yin energy.

Fun Schway Journal

NOTES - comments:

Fun Schway Journal

Maintaining Balance

From the ancient teachings of Feng Shui, positive and negative energies surround us within the environment, nature, situations, relationships and material products. Be mindful of Yin/Yang energy by paying attention to details, and then create a positive, healthy lifestyle by recording these differences. Note the time, date (similarities) of repetitive negative situations that require attention and you will attract positive energy: maintaining the balance: Good Fun Schway!

Date:_____

Gratitude: for the positive Yang energy.

Awareness: negative Yin energy.

Fun Schway Journal

NOTES - comments:

Fun Schway Journal

Maintaining Balance

From the ancient teachings of Feng Shui, positive and negative energies surround us within the environment, nature, situations, relationships and material products. Be mindful of Yin/Yang energy by paying attention to details, and then create a positive, healthy lifestyle by recording these differences. Note the time, date (similarities) of repetitive negative situations that require attention and you will attract positive energy: maintaining the balance: Good Fun Schway!

Date:_____

Gratitude: for the positive Yang energy.

Awareness: negative Yin energy.

Fun Schway Journal

NOTES - comments:

Fun Schway Journal

Maintaining Balance

From the ancient teachings of Feng Shui, positive and negative energies surround us within the environment, nature, situations, relationships and material products. Be mindful of Yin/Yang energy by paying attention to details, and then create a positive, healthy lifestyle by recording these differences. Note the time, date (similarities) of repetitive negative situations that require attention and you will attract positive energy: maintaining the balance: Good Fun Schway!

Date:_____

Gratitude: for the positive Yang energy.

Awareness: negative Yin energy.

Fun Schway Journal

NOTES - comments:

Fun Schway Journal

Maintaining Balance

From the ancient teachings of Feng Shui, positive and negative energies surround us within the environment, nature, situations, relationships and material products. Be mindful of Yin/Yang energy by paying attention to details, and then create a positive, healthy lifestyle by recording these differences. Note the time, date (similarities) of repetitive negative situations that require attention and you will attract positive energy: maintaining the balance: Good Fun Schway!

Date:_____

Gratitude: for the positive Yang energy.

Awareness: negative Yin energy.

Fun Schway Journal

NOTES - comments:

Fun Schway Journal

Maintaining Balance

From the ancient teachings of Feng Shui, positive and negative energies surround us within the environment, nature, situations, relationships and material products. Be mindful of Yin/Yang energy by paying attention to details, and then create a positive, healthy lifestyle by recording these differences. Note the time, date (similarities) of repetitive negative situations that require attention and you will attract positive energy: maintaining the balance: Good Fun Schway!

Date:_____

Gratitude: for the positive Yang energy.

Awareness: negative Yin energy.

Fun Schway Journal

NOTES - comments:

Fun Schway Journal

Maintaining Balance

From the ancient teachings of Feng Shui, positive and negative energies surround us within the environment, nature, situations, relationships and material products. Be mindful of Yin/Yang energy by paying attention to details, and then create a positive, healthy lifestyle by recording these differences. Note the time, date (similarities) of repetitive negative situations that require attention and you will attract positive energy: maintaining the balance: Good Fun Schway!

Date:_____

Gratitude: for the positive Yang energy.

Awareness: negative Yin energy.

Fun Schway Journal

NOTES - comments:

Fun Schway Journal

Maintaining Balance

From the ancient teachings of Feng Shui, positive and negative energies surround us within the environment, nature, situations, relationships and material products. Be mindful of Yin/Yang energy by paying attention to details, and then create a positive, healthy lifestyle by recording these differences. Note the time, date (similarities) of repetitive negative situations that require attention and you will attract positive energy: maintaining the balance: Good Fun Schway!

Date:_____

Gratitude: for the positive Yang energy.

Awareness: negative Yin energy.

Fun Schway Journal

NOTES - comments:

Fun Schway Journal

Maintaining Balance

From the ancient teachings of Feng Shui, positive and negative energies surround us within the environment, nature, situations, relationships and material products. Be mindful of Yin/Yang energy by paying attention to details, and then create a positive, healthy lifestyle by recording these differences. Note the time, date (similarities) of repetitive negative situations that require attention and you will attract positive energy: maintaining the balance: Good Fun Schway!

Date:_____

Gratitude: for the positive Yang energy.

Awareness: negative Yin energy.

Fun Schway Journal

NOTES - comments:

Fun Schway Journal

Maintaining Balance

From the ancient teachings of Feng Shui, positive and negative energies surround us within the environment, nature, situations, relationships and material products. Be mindful of Yin/Yang energy by paying attention to details, and then create a positive, healthy lifestyle by recording these differences. Note the time, date (similarities) of repetitive negative situations that require attention and you will attract positive energy: maintaining the balance: Good Fun Schway!

Date:_____

Gratitude: for the positive Yang energy.

Awareness: negative Yin energy.

Fun Schway Journal

NOTES - comments:

Fun Schway Journal

Maintaining Balance

From the ancient teachings of Feng Shui, positive and negative energies surround us within the environment, nature, situations, relationships and material products. Be mindful of Yin/Yang energy by paying attention to details, and then create a positive, healthy lifestyle by recording these differences. Note the time, date (similarities) of repetitive negative situations that require attention and you will attract positive energy: maintaining the balance: Good Fun Schway!

Date:_____

Gratitude: for the positive Yang energy.

Awareness: negative Yin energy.

Fun Schway Journal

NOTES - comments:

Fun Schway Journal

Maintaining Balance

From the ancient teachings of Feng Shui, positive and negative energies surround us within the environment, nature, situations, relationships and material products. Be mindful of Yin/Yang energy by paying attention to details, and then create a positive, healthy lifestyle by recording these differences. Note the time, date (similarities) of repetitive negative situations that require attention and you will attract positive energy: maintaining the balance: Good Fun Schway!

Date:_____

Gratitude: for the positive Yang energy.

Awareness: negative Yin energy.

Fun Schway Journal

NOTES - comments:

Fun Schway Journal

Maintaining Balance

From the ancient teachings of Feng Shui, positive and negative energies surround us within the environment, nature, situations, relationships and material products. Be mindful of Yin/Yang energy by paying attention to details, and then create a positive, healthy lifestyle by recording these differences. Note the time, date (similarities) of repetitive negative situations that require attention and you will attract positive energy: maintaining the balance: Good Fun Schway!

Date:_____

Gratitude: for the positive Yang energy.

Awareness: negative Yin energy.

Fun Schway Journal

NOTES - comments:

Fun Schway Journal

Maintaining Balance

From the ancient teachings of Feng Shui, positive and negative energies surround us within the environment, nature, situations, relationships and material products. Be mindful of Yin/Yang energy by paying attention to details, and then create a positive, healthy lifestyle by recording these differences. Note the time, date (similarities) of repetitive negative situations that require attention and you will attract positive energy: maintaining the balance: Good Fun Schway!

Date:_____

Gratitude: for the positive Yang energy.

Awareness: negative Yin energy.

Fun Schway Journal

NOTES - comments:

Fun Schway Journal

Maintaining Balance

From the ancient teachings of Feng Shui, positive and negative energies surround us within the environment, nature, situations, relationships and material products. Be mindful of Yin/Yang energy by paying attention to details, and then create a positive, healthy lifestyle by recording these differences. Note the time, date (similarities) of repetitive negative situations that require attention and you will attract positive energy: maintaining the balance: Good Fun Schway!

Date:_____

Gratitude: for the positive Yang energy.

Awareness: negative Yin energy.

Fun Schway Journal

NOTES - comments:

Fun Schway Journal

Maintaining Balance

From the ancient teachings of Feng Shui, positive and negative energies surround us within the environment, nature, situations, relationships and material products. Be mindful of Yin/Yang energy by paying attention to details, and then create a positive, healthy lifestyle by recording these differences. Note the time, date (similarities) of repetitive negative situations that require attention and you will attract positive energy: maintaining the balance: Good Fun Schway!

Date:_____

Gratitude: for the positive Yang energy.

Awareness: negative Yin energy.

Fun Schway Journal

NOTES - comments:

Fun Schway Journal

Maintaining Balance

From the ancient teachings of Feng Shui, positive and negative energies surround us within the environment, nature, situations, relationships and material products. Be mindful of Yin/Yang energy by paying attention to details, and then create a positive, healthy lifestyle by recording these differences. Note the time, date (similarities) of repetitive negative situations that require attention and you will attract positive energy: maintaining the balance: Good Fun Schway!

Date:_____

Gratitude: for the positive Yang energy.

Awareness: negative Yin energy.

Fun Schway Journal

NOTES - comments:

Fun Schway Journal

Maintaining Balance

From the ancient teachings of Feng Shui, positive and negative energies surround us within the environment, nature, situations, relationships and material products. Be mindful of Yin/Yang energy by paying attention to details, and then create a positive, healthy lifestyle by recording these differences. Note the time, date (similarities) of repetitive negative situations that require attention and you will attract positive energy: maintaining the balance: Good Fun Schway!

Date:_____

Gratitude: for the positive Yang energy.

Awareness: negative Yin energy.

Fun Schway Journal

NOTES - comments:

Fun Schway Journal

Maintaining Balance

From the ancient teachings of Feng Shui, positive and negative energies surround us within the environment, nature, situations, relationships and material products. Be mindful of Yin/Yang energy by paying attention to details, and then create a positive, healthy lifestyle by recording these differences. Note the time, date (similarities) of repetitive negative situations that require attention and you will attract positive energy: maintaining the balance: Good Fun Schway!

Date:_____

Gratitude: for the positive Yang energy.

Awareness: negative Yin energy.

Fun Schway Journal

NOTES - comments:

Fun Schway Journal

Maintaining Balance

From the ancient teachings of Feng Shui, positive and negative energies surround us within the environment, nature, situations, relationships and material products. Be mindful of Yin/Yang energy by paying attention to details, and then create a positive, healthy lifestyle by recording these differences. Note the time, date (similarities) of repetitive negative situations that require attention and you will attract positive energy: maintaining the balance: Good Fun Schway!

Date:_____

Gratitude: for the positive Yang energy.

Awareness: negative Yin energy.

Fun Schway Journal

NOTES - comments:

Fun Schway Journal

Maintaining Balance

From the ancient teachings of Feng Shui, positive and negative energies surround us within the environment, nature, situations, relationships and material products. Be mindful of Yin/Yang energy by paying attention to details, and then create a positive, healthy lifestyle by recording these differences. Note the time, date (similarities) of repetitive negative situations that require attention and you will attract positive energy: maintaining the balance: Good Fun Schway!

Date:_____

Gratitude: for the positive Yang energy.

Awareness: negative Yin energy.

Fun Schway Journal

NOTES - comments:

Fun Schway Journal

Maintaining Balance

From the ancient teachings of Feng Shui, positive and negative energies surround us within the environment, nature, situations, relationships and material products. Be mindful of Yin/Yang energy by paying attention to details, and then create a positive, healthy lifestyle by recording these differences. Note the time, date (similarities) of repetitive negative situations that require attention and you will attract positive energy: maintaining the balance: Good Fun Schway!

Date:_____

Gratitude: for the positive Yang energy.

Awareness: negative Yin energy.

Fun Schway Journal

NOTES - comments:

Fun Schway Journal

Maintaining Balance

From the ancient teachings of Feng Shui, positive and negative energies surround us within the environment, nature, situations, relationships and material products. Be mindful of Yin/Yang energy by paying attention to details, and then create a positive, healthy lifestyle by recording these differences. Note the time, date (similarities) of repetitive negative situations that require attention and you will attract positive energy: maintaining the balance: Good Fun Schway!

Date:_____

Gratitude: for the positive Yang energy.

Awareness: negative Yin energy.

Fun Schway Journal

NOTES - comments:

Fun Schway Journal

Maintaining Balance

From the ancient teachings of Feng Shui, positive and negative energies surround us within the environment, nature, situations, relationships and material products. Be mindful of Yin/Yang energy by paying attention to details, and then create a positive, healthy lifestyle by recording these differences. Note the time, date (similarities) of repetitive negative situations that require attention and you will attract positive energy: maintaining the balance: Good Fun Schway!

Date:_____

Gratitude: for the positive Yang energy.

Awareness: negative Yin energy.

Fun Schway Journal

NOTES - comments:

Fun Schway Journal

Maintaining Balance

From the ancient teachings of Feng Shui, positive and negative energies surround us within the environment, nature, situations, relationships and material products. Be mindful of Yin/Yang energy by paying attention to details, and then create a positive, healthy lifestyle by recording these differences. Note the time, date (similarities) of repetitive negative situations that require attention and you will attract positive energy: maintaining the balance: Good Fun Schway!

Date:_____

Gratitude: for the positive Yang energy.

Awareness: negative Yin energy.

Fun Schway Journal

NOTES - comments:

Fun Schway Journal

Maintaining Balance

From the ancient teachings of Feng Shui, positive and negative energies surround us within the environment, nature, situations, relationships and material products. Be mindful of Yin/Yang energy by paying attention to details, and then create a positive, healthy lifestyle by recording these differences. Note the time, date (similarities) of repetitive negative situations that require attention and you will attract positive energy: maintaining the balance: Good Fun Schway!

Date:_____

Gratitude: for the positive Yang energy.

Awareness: negative Yin energy.

Fun Schway Journal

Fun Schway Journal

Maintaining Balance

From the ancient teachings of Feng Shui, positive and negative energies surround us within the environment, nature, situations, relationships and material products. Be mindful of Yin/Yang energy by paying attention to details, and then create a positive, healthy lifestyle by recording these differences. Note the time, date (similarities) of repetitive negative situations that require attention and you will attract positive energy: maintaining the balance: Good Fun Schway!

~ * ~

Journaling
is an amazing way to learn about yourself,
your likes and dislikes, your positive and negative attractions
and your ability to develop a clearer picture of your
strengths and weaknesses.

Use it for gratitude when positive energy surrounds you.
(Items, places, people, colors, situations, buildings,
weather, foods, music, etc)
Use it to identify negative situations,
relationships & environments.
The Yin/Yang observations will allow you to change,
remove or recognize any positive or negative
repetitive factors to...
Maintain Balance ~ Feng Shui .

~ * ~

Fun Schway Journal

~ * ~

Author – Mallory Neeve Wilkins

Professional Interior Designer specializing in Feng Shui uses journaling both with clients and for herself to motivate and maintain balance. Believing that by following the path of positive and negative energies you will improve your lifestyle, relationships, creativity, career and health.

~ * ~

Made in the USA
Charleston, SC
18 December 2015